Second Edition, 2025
ISBN: 979-8-218-74413-7

Edited by Tilghman Alexander Goldsborough
Cover Design by Montana James Thomas & Tilghman Alexander Goldsborough
Layout Design by Sonae White
Assistant Layout Design by Montana James Thomas
Typeset in Dante, Brondi Condensed, Snell Roundhand

CONCERNING *the* *Dinner*

Preface

It's so beautifully arranged on the plate, you know someone's fingers have been all over it.

—Julia Child

CONCERNING THE DINNER

Montana James Thomas

TABLE OF CONTENTS

Slinging Objects

Pearl poppers sucking on oysters under awnings
or marinating raw things in their open-concept kitchens.
Young like buildings, big like cock.
They'll order martinis and something bubbly like we all would,
like we all would volunteer to pick their scalps,
monkey-happy and peckish.
These things don't happen randomly as kitchen sink dinners do —

so for starters, the juice of burdock,
the lamb neck, the vegan in his bed of celeriac mash, the hearty loaf,
for dessert, the clam Tartufo,
the deconstructed spotted dick,
the juice of carrot- floating
in whipped brandy cream.
It's on her lip as she laughs in agreement- her nod exciting and easy like
aspic—
the smile that launched a thousand dollars worth of fish eggs,
an ugly rich woman-to-be, no doubt. Sipping toast in the carcass of
Cafe Petrossian.

Suntan of love

Girls day,
bacon face,
tits out,
hair hat, bleaching under the sun up on the tower's roof.
Shimmy, do the mashed potato, shining, laying out,
beating giggles from each cheek at the floating geese below—

a curl pushing lovelock onlooker spots her,
sweet in his brow, sweat in his tunic, a lily on his brooch,
got his meat hard, cock for breakfast, alarm
clock,
wake up, Ashleigh.
He aims his arrows and releases;

That's one! That's two! That's three!
Bullseye.

He's killed her three songbirds for to
pluck bare, and eat up,
as an appetizer to the main event,

hurricane stew for her
nerve,
boots and bandaids and dirt dragged along and ladled from rivers of
downpour
for her nerve,
lightening to the turret
for her rattling little nerve,
her silly little shaky hands— next time:

A l'Orange

Am I the fool or am I the funniest girl in the French court?
Should I be stomped out for the sake of forests?
Here's a bouquet, it smells like garlic, it's slow cooking at eight hundred and
fifty degrees.
I'm tapping my foot
at a dead duck.

Right this way

I used to think robbers knew they were robbers,
how I'm just a pile of wigs like I said I would be,
now I'm just a pile of pool sharks,
I'm just a red-meat-eating cow,
the room turns blue in agreement.

Jumping out of our sleep to a loud crash,
looking around, stunned, like two drowsy meerkats.
Where did that come from?
What is it that will be for breakfast?

The cartoonist

My Little Cow, isn't the world a lovely place?
Salted,
like butter that is salted.
Natural, like a calendar when it's July and the photo is of a barn,
Or November when it's of a
wrestler.

Piles of core, of center,
scattered ores of plain earth,
living together like ghosts on the hardwood floor.
A surprise flake of sea salt is just a stone, after all— cold and still.

I come from a stickier school; one with funny horns,
smiling around in here, feeling like a butterball on a maroon tablecloth, in
some dim velvet restaurant, the server rushing over to clean up crumbs with
one of those fabulous metal scoopy things –

I know the paw or stab or divine pepper shaker to trade,
I know which caramels to
offer him —

Animals are angels
and men are creatures who need, more than anyone, to have their hair
played with.
You can run a marathon for a good cause,
but New York dust
never goes away.

Beer battered and slathered in sauce

Your patch of onion grass,
who knows if it tastes better or worse
than the three-thousand-year-old honey sitting in tombs that the scientists
say is
perfectly edible.
I'll never taste either because
it's too expensive to steal
from kings.

I like boys who have colors around them,
shrines of plastic puppy figures,
gummy stars and shells on their neck stubble,
tiny paper windmills on their ears.
It's nice to know that I'm a little rainbow bauble
but
I still wanna get hit by a bus.

I'll just hang around your thumb,
or string your shoelace through my empty part
and dangle around down there,

and I don't wanna be anybody's novel sober evening,
so please, by all means, get blackout,
and I wanna bomb AA,
so let me taste it on your mouth too.

There's also an ice cream machine

It slid thick down the mountain over children and spoons and dogs.
Incense was lit
and immediately snuffed during the takeover. That bright, deep, spit,
overcooking the terrors,
kept mom with her frying pan,
kept up the cookie jar,
they both slept in and stayed forever,
"Just layers in the cake now," the newscaster said of clouds.

Oh, Canada

Ask your socks what time it is
and they'll just roll their eyes. Ask your underwear,
and they'll pass you the mustard.
Close your eyes and think of Vancouver,
emerging from a shadow, he was eating a sandwich,
he pressed it down so respectfully. Like popping in dentures.
Stacks of colorful jewels, searchlights in the the thick, low, smog —
I'd prefer something fizzy, but I'll take a big fat lemon,
It's juice,
running down my throat like stinging nettle grazing the backpack of
a podcaster as he makes his way through the foggy hills of eastern
Kentucky.
Astonished by the day,
mind boggled by the night,
nodding at the cold and digging the heat,
a survey of everything and yet
absolutely nothing to eat.

Grape grape grape

80801ADN pinky pop kitty,
it's so much more than pie, it's all of China,
vast and rounded,
spatchcocked, doubled,
and laid flat,
diced and stacked like blocks for children
and men,
a market helping
at market price.
purple and silver foil plated
for eating,
sour and viscous red syrup
for sticking.

God watches us dream and forget and go about our routines
every single day,
unless dreams are the one private experience..

peering through the keyhole — it thinks to itself,
"Don't care how long I have to wait. I like it in the rain or in the winter
time."
while aloud it can only utter, in a clotted breath, "Kill James"

Powder room

Sometimes for looking, water sits below me today.
To drink it in is to swim in it, but today I am just watching
as glazed chunks of sturdy flatware,
thick shards that crumble themselves
like a clogged foot at the opera,
crash against the shore,
concrete and pre-war.

I spent all dawn moving around in his hacked chips,
sitting at the bottom of the thing, the tub,
shaking them off, flicking my tan line, explicit in his mother's late mother's
bathroom,
or on his late father's tarmac roof, saluting planes, swallowing him alive,
dripping in some proof of summer's end,

but this afternoon I'm just sitting atop and scraping,
like the glints on a wave — the tiny silver screen can-can dancers in sparkling
swimwear and head caps,
capsizing and recovering over and over, while flutes and strings cradle the
white noise of guest-list-bongo.

A red low moon had floated in the pale and strong west coast search beams
of Brooklyn,
as I rose into becoming whatever crowded bouquet sat still between your
chest and your armpit, don't be ridiculous, it was tuberose,
it was so certainly tuberose— can't you see? can't you smell? can't you taste?

a body brought to you by oil slick brought
to you by the plumber sitting on his head with a doll in his left pocket,
a wrench, that's me,
and a poodle, Isabelle, nipping at his right,
also me, me too, same
yapping for a sip,
for a tilt over into the bowl,
to lap up whatever concerning surface tension sits eagerly in porcelain.

Beef Stroganoff

Whether or not you are disgusted by reaching into a sink full of dirty dishwater, clogged with bits of food, is a choice you make. I, being such a good person, have chosen not to be disgusted by it.

There's a good boy, here's his treat.

Spaghetti eat dog

A man on the train sits,
unremarkable, wearing a Boston t-shirt.
Cut my head off, stuff with boom boom,
raw fish,
whipped cream,
sugar bow,
on a bed of greens, on a plate of silver.
Serve it fresh and hot to the other passengers—
to Dandy and Doggy and
Sticky Toffee Maniac and Red Nose Panty Hose Library Cock Fire,
for them to stroke and tear and eat like piggies,
but with their hands.
Pig eat pig.
Nancy in bifocals reaching for my cheek.
Guy gets his slice, Joey is a hair freak.
Some loony prick hops on at 23rd,
rolled up newspaper
for beating.
He beat the steam right out of the thing.
My body,
long gone,
got off
at Essex.

The King's jam party

He slapped raspberry jam across the table and screamed, for he was but three years old.

Pain du jour

I'm going to the Spanish restaurant like we used to do to do
wine straight to the mouth to the sound of
nothing.
Messages from mommy in scraps of restaurant table cloth,
wet the fork, trace your shape, tear it out.
Sweet little tosses- no bats, no boys, just men
with plates of Mole and bread baskets, back when bread was served at dinner.
They'd watch her sink with me,
my tail wagging at her,
they watched that too. And as for eternity,
the Mole sat thick and still around whatever hunk would come with it.

Now, in some tower
I'm going to the next shopping mall for good and for juice.
Baccarat, dog piss, white asparagus soup.
What do you call that? Pain du jour?

He cups his hand and strokes my hair,
boys in poses line his walls
and I've got something gel-coated on my handle
and the top of me is full of bristles
and I'm sitting here waiting
and it's always a little damp.
So what do you want from me?
I'm nothing but a toothbrush after all,
at least for this David,
at least for a couple.

Flavor store

Tip-toeing across the searchlight,
picking up her bottle, spraying it on her neck in her mouth on her cock in
the bath on the phone on her back on her bed on her own on her pillow, wet,
Kind of Valley of the Dolls kind of
'see, you've got your diphenhydramine.'
he keeps spotting things out in my mind like a clock,
diphenhydramine, diphenhydramine, diphenhydramine
and you came up in Paco Rabanne and you came up at the deli
in a flat plastic squeezer with three separate suckers each full-ish of different
sour flavors.

Omelette, you like?

Hand-carved Geisha in my bar of soap, worn down, begins to resemble the silhouette of a cowboy.
Bathroom window brag, bidet just sitting there in the light. He's obsessed with my breakfast.

A Foggy Day In London Town

A foggy day in London Town,
exchanging squints with haircuts
and bay windows.
The British Museum had lost
it's charm.
The Great British Bake Off had lost
it's charm.

Underbaked,
and the inside will end up sloppy,
or worse, it will collapse.
Over-baked,
and the outside could crack,
and break off completely.

Dear Horsemen, cool your ramps quickly in an ice bath

Puppies also die,
and yet,
they don't stoically reserve themselves like The New York Times recipe for
Grilled Salmon with Mustard Glaze.
They're smart for just looking and jumping,
only speak dumbly at them if you really must.
Come with me,
and we will drink our fill
of the milk of the white goat.
There's nothing 'good' about that 'girl'
she won't leave it or bring it or
sit and that's
fine by
me.

John Dory

She is delivered directly to The King's gates.
full of gin, there she goes,
across his drawbridge, over his glowing moat.
Handbells and beeswax,
a warm nighttime welcoming for the catch in question,
which dangles in her grip,
her fragrant iridescent ransom ready to be
sliced.

Onto the dish
and down The King's throat it goes,
delicious and boneless.
Her pearls bump up against each other,
'Exquisite,
your highness!'

Under the table,
resting on her lap,
her iPhone dings
and illuminates her tits,
'Whatsup, bitch'
The tumbling English breeze in his French sails,
the death of his downtown, the inventor of his
silly
little
fish.

After savory nibbles at the wine bar

she was driving home
down the highway,
buzzing like a monkey.
She got rear-ended by some loser.
They made quite the pileup for themselves.
Where one car was bent, the other stuck its snout and
breathed.
The impact knocked the diamond right out of her head.
Four police cars, two fire trucks
and three ambulances-
their flashlights scanned the dark fields lining the highway,
lit up from all angles like The 4th
came early,
but no sign of her left earning anywhere.

Sing it, Ella!

A dog howls at sirens that drive by,
I want
my neighbor's steak
and a glass of vino.

She itches her trachea with each
note.
All that meat and no potatoes
just ain't right—

my nose up against the wall that we share,
a small lump on her neck,
she calls her doctor and asks for
his help.

Not a chicken bone, silly,
a tumor,

don't
worry.

Cow's famous milk

Electric mixer in hand,
she stares into her sink of stainless steel.
Matadors flung flat onto the wall behind her like spaghetti.

She exhales and begins to scrub the whisks,
she remembers her husband and how he was badly hurt.
He got hit and was paralyzed from the hips down,
but now he lifts weights every day
and poses for big muscle mags,
good for him.

The night they met
they were at a friend's small gathering,
dancing next to each other like two same-sex birds,
no alcohol.
This felt kind of weird and sad in a hot way. She remembers his nothing.

Mixer washed and dripping dry, she moves to the next piece,
a fabulous, costly knife.

In the city of Pittsburgh, Pennsylvania

BJ drove a truck fueled by peanut oil and kept her fridge fully stocked with
unpasteurized cow's milk.
She, like most others, died in the big one. If only the earth could have
fossilized
her cloud of french fry car exhaust and the way she walked from her
driveway to the kitchen,
but alas,
just crumbs.

Her sister survived the big one, and now she wanders across the jungle with
a list of three things:

Butter
Progresso
Laundry

Her list is too small and the jungle is too
big,
and her car keys?
Buried.
And her friends?
Dead as rocks.
And her rations?
Goose eggs.
And her pet puppy
decided
it wanted to see the new world.

Something something, a maiden's heartache

Interrupt the butter churner! Scream, "Oh no you don't!" and then just
scream, "Ah!"— like a kind of normal scream. Then shove her off the
side of the porch and take the milk inside the house. Slam the door. It's
snowing outside and the camera pulls back and the house is becoming
smaller, and the butter churner lay crying in the snow with a bloody nose,
weeping toward the sky. Her wails echo across the countryside of central
Pennsylvania, becoming louder and louder as she becomes smaller and
smaller on the screen. The screen goes black and ending credits
begin.
Inside the purple kitchen, the very naughty kitty, twelve feet tall and
standing on his hind legs, smiles widely down at the milk. It shines back up
into his eyes. His friendly fangs peek out. His name is Fred and he's a grave
robber, and he hasn't had such a treat in
ages.
We mix cereal into it— colorful marshmallow shapes. We can eat these
thingies! We could even throw them in the air like glitter or across the table
like dice if we'd like to. I guess I chose simply to eat them, but what did you
expect me to do? I was a mouse then, for a moment, in fear and in awe. I
found places to host me through the winter, like a spot under the butcher's
block; or a spot under the porch, safe from snow but with light from
between planks; or a spot at the foot of the master bed at night some hours
'fore the master woke. He didn't have to know and he never did.
I watched him eat: his long tongue, his hard whiskers, and his rounded
cheeks. I drank milk from his splash and ate rainbow crumbs from his
play.

Eloise

Took my hood off to smoke,
pass it back and forth, avoiding the cover,
lines of enterers, ropes of cum.

You came in my eye when I asked you to cum in my mouth and I was so
mad, but I guess I can't complain.
What if I was born into water instead of a bed, instead of a magazine that
doesn't know my name?

Child karate chopped the steak,
God bless him,
Keep eating, faggot.
We will not say goodbye until he's been tongued.
Come back and kiss me, faggot,
on my spit slit of animatronic pulse.
Walk through those bears,
those big helpful Marys, those horrible creatures who
the bartenders
are not nice enough to kill.

They are too kind. Thumping and nodding behind cock.
They eat people who cry. They kill people who do not plan.
You're just a subscription service.
Welcome to my unfortunate smell.

The way it melts

Where do they go when their eyes are closed?
Is nothing wind-beaten anymore? Not even the actress in front of a fan,
making up blush like the milk frother on Sunday?
Best have your Englishman take you home then.
He walks off screen and into the woods.

Keep it short, toots

Please, God,
Some monarch,
weeping on his dainty little knees,
Wagner, Marie Antoinette, and residue of some bite-sized foie-gras-puff-
pastry-monstrosity
fill up his various
holes, respectively.
Hands in prayer, he begs for it — "Sis, your wig looks good."

He is well-lit in his theater-mansion, he is a faggot, and he will die — it will
be unclear whether his death was a murder or a suicide.

His money will go
to the museums.

Dinner party

Hello, little chickie, you taste so good, you're so hot when you look up at me like that. Your skin is golden and smells delicious and will melt in my mouth. I will eat you and I will eat your children and then I will cry. It feels so good, I'm so full of you. I'm so fed up with you.

Christian the 7th

It's early morning and men line the sidewalks, hosing their buildings,
wetting the soil of the West Village.
So many spunk trees,
so much tree spunk in the air,
and nary a fruit bearer to catch it.
A chef over the stove, peppering the soup, baby in arm.
Baby boy sneezes for luck and some flavor.
No more beating the baby boy, just stroking his hair above the heat of the
kitchen.
What a brilliant little genius, and with no words to suck on and with no teeth
to chew for
and with chopped foods below him and with daddy in chef pants.

Tomato plant

Dead?

Seikilos Epitaph

Two couples were dining outside under an umbrella at an Italian restaurant in the West Village around 2:00 pm. One of the women was coughing into her hands. Her husband pounded her rounded back with his flat firm palm again and again and again and again to help. Her small breathy coughs, like speed bumps over the penne, became increasingly fainter as she continued to curl in. The other woman politely asked the waiter, "Could you bring us a thing of water please?" Finally, the woman stopped coughing and her head fell to the plate, still and silent. The husband stopped pounding her back and they all looked around at each other in shock. An angry man in a car driving by the restaurant honked his horn for about five whole seconds at a bike that got into his lane. The husband then slowly reached over and lifted her head by her chin and her ponytail. She was certainly dead and her face was caked in vodka sauce and some wilted basil. One lone penne had managed to stick to her ear. He began to move her mouth like a puppet as if she were speaking and making noises— like cow noises and bird noises. They all broke into smiles. The other wife jumped up and moved her limp arms from behind. They all laughed as they pretended she was dancing and singing La Bamba. Her husband got food all over his hands. They topped her off with wine on the head. They drank and laughed so hard that their cheeks were red and their abdomens were sore. The waiter, Joe, brought over whipped cream, with which they could also play. Oh to lunch on a Wednesday.

Food grade

Cut me up like chicken sometime,
throw me onto myself,
my fresh cold jumbo shrimps,
I'm the Barbie.

Freedom Forrest

The smell of oranges and rugs —
"Your great grandfather would shoot arrows at the ceiling," she said, "this
year we'll mount the Christmas tree upside down on the ceiling and invite
that aunt of yours to help decorate it."

In New York his downstairs neighbor bled out entirely and sat there for five
days.
It's now been a month since they removed the body, and the landlord has yet
to tend to the incredible amount of blood.
It has soaked into the wood and stained it, they'll have to re-floor the place.
And as the blood sits there, it cooks in the heat of that sunny August living
room.

"It smells like a butcher shop," he says, beginning his ascent up the stairs
  and toward his apartment, "I'll open my windows and yank out my hair,"
weeping into his packages "I'll go to the beach."

Iconic Makeover

Modeling's my dream and I'm not gonna let anything get in the way of that.
It's very cut-throat, one must be hasty and beeswax-like; one must be
Something Evans or Charlize Theron or add a little sugar.
Dig deep enough and your poodle will be cleaning strudel off of murder
weapons hidden under grass on some side field in the North Woods.
A perfect square of turf flung up by Sparky, revealing a simple silver blade,
slicked with blood, still sparkling.

Mark by Mark by Mark by Mark by Mocha Choca

Nowadays,
we walk into a room and face-play with our guts,
I eat lots of hummus,
I hear ghosts in the hallway at night.
That's all very well, and I agree ; it'll have to be eggshells.
I slay
I ride horses,
I eat soup soup,
I hear loud noises at night,
I hear like a sort of creak in the hallway
but not like a floor-creak,
well,
not just like a floor-creak, but also a kinda soft shuffling thump like someone
picking something up or trying to silently grab a set of keys caught beneath
objects in the dark.
There's another one—
I just heard a sound that sounded like someone giving a go at a lock or gently
testing a doorknob,
or flipping a light switch up and down three times to see if it's really out.
I hear, lowly in the walls,
touching me through my pillow,
the upstairs neighbor's tv.

New York hearts me

I guess I love New Jersey now,
Car wash equals hose plus whipped cream minus motor divided by muscle.
I'm just a fluffer,
turns out I've always been, and I think I've finally got the hang of it:
You see, it's mostly just poodles and lions
drooling for the gods,
all the rest is sparkle.

Apparently, parasites were found breeding in a shower stall at the Equinox on
Orchard Street,
you can't make this shit up:
Thin, slimy, black, worm-like forms entangled and pulsing-
as soon as the witness's damp flip flop touched the tile to approach them
they scurried and slid into the cracks in the wall, toward the steam room.

But otherwise, the city feels large today,
big and bright and it smells like candy cane,
helicopters overhead scanning for the culprit,
you're always a block away from the latest shooting,
and I'm always alone when I smell my first cum tree of the spring.
What a lovely day to be ourselves.

Horndog cornball

Gone like butter.
Zipped up like a puffer,
whip it out already,
s t u d!
Throw the Diet Coke inside of me and slap it off my lip,
s t u d!
Put me,
blue and wet,
on the stove,

you doggy!

Jam your foot
into my barking mouth—
say less,
gorgeous!
Diet coke goes through me fast, it knows just what to do,
escape the fire,
get out into the rain,
into the gutter—
gone forever.

The Plaza Hotel

We bumped props under a crooked moon dangling in the popup sky.
Flicking his crown of hay above me in the dark grass,
the park made into a set by yellow lamps.
We queued her fabulous entrance:

Swinging down and across the stage on a rope like the bandit of our dreams,
"Tomorrow!", she sang in a high E sharp,
at the belly of her swoop she dusted the hardwood,
and with her sword
beheaded my robin, kissing my nose as she did,
collecting her coins

and those of the countryside —

for the bats and the swimming pool lights, and the faggot who sleeps in the
hot soil of the vineyard,
and the ugly chambermaid, all cauliflower ears and nose, administering her
masters opium intravenously,
and the morning geese, and the gunshots,
and her fingernails, scrubbed clean in the river's cold and clear.

Her wrapped wrists,
her filthy teeth,
she took my robin's head,
cut short.
My robin, all headless above me now,
glowing green clouds, like machine fog, racing across this new indigo
opening.

Salad Niçoise

Speak roughly to your little boy
and beat him when he sneezes.
Say grace, you brilliant little dingbat!
Those gorgeous painted dishes,

that elegant sturdy Pipestone China
flying across the room and breaking.
There's trouble in that there cupboard,

every champagne flute in it
quivers as the hour hand threatens to strike

dinner time.

Kentucky

A week ago I was in the shower and I remembered how when I was young I was fascinated with tornados and other natural disasters. I was in the middle of asking someone questions about tornados and because he didn't know how to answer, he thought he would try and make me laugh so he yelled "Texas Titty Twisters!" while pinching my nipple and twisting it. That was the first time I ever got a Texas Titty Twister.

Peggy's usual

Something preposterous and '40s-ish, like
red hot alphabet pasta pie,
was sitting in the backseat trying to frame her, and then

she sat in it
while getting in the car,
and for the entire drive home.

The pasta looked like jello in
red on her thigh hair,
spelling things under her on the next sharp turn,
cream on the upholstery.

"She would have wanted you to have this," I say, dabbing dry my eyes and
handing him my finger.

I likely won't really take a bus to Cleveland this winter

for the sake of seeing some guy, but I might.
I'll most certainly threaten to.
Strapping on the chest you'll need for December,
pledging allegiance for the grace of God,
his green grass on a hill on a map on a piece of paper on a lazy Susan.
Oh my,
maybe even slamming against the air as a secret dessert,
silent and on fire. A ditched guilty couch among the frosted tips of Jersey
woods, candy stripes,
teenagers will light it up and dive into ice behind the wall of smoke they've
made.
Scrubbing the sugar into a deep itch on my hip…
Bombe
Alaska,
let's,
immediately.

Nothing left to watch on TV

He took a sip and proceeded to simmer me in oil and chopped garlic. He then added a generous splash of dry white wine, before topping up his glass. He gently pawed at me with a wooden spoon for a while, scooting me around in the hot pan. Adding salt and pepper, he continued to do so, occasionally dancing with his shoulders, neck, and feet to the faint music; occasionally shaking the pan by its handle so I would slide around, getting me nice and coated. He leaned in, smelled me, and then smiled down at me. I laid there on the stove looking up at him—those bright, blasé stars, as swell as ever.

Strip

A man, belly down
on the chalky morning sidewalk,
might be dead—
wake up bluebirds, it's time for a full, juicy day of work!
A terrific year for this variety, indeed— peck,
and peck hard for your family,
nest into the swankiest oak by The Boathouse and
dump your eggs.

See them? They spin their sugar into fluff,
and those ones over there trained themselves to spit incredibly far,
and those ones over there trained their children to spit even further.
Nudging the stroller, as if it needed more work,
Cheers to the horses!
And the kids, how they've grown.

At night Central Park is stage lit.
Crown your superstar, mommy, hopping from this lighting to
that,
purple Gatorade and citronella escaping from under the stage door of the
Delecorte Theater,
pine clusters sweating in the dark heat like Julian in math class,
he was tall for his age
and smelled bad
and they all laughed incessantly.

Service

It doesn't really pay
to eat three meals a day,
and it certainly doesn't pay
to call one of them breakfast.

Don't work that way

350 degrees my ass.
There's a jaguar in your kitchen cabinet spying on you,
he caught you eating my birthday cake,
and he caught you smiling about it.

Week of March:
Pound cake.
Week of April:
Raspberry earl gray blondies.

Let's fire our bosses
together,
and you can pour beer into my mouth from above,

slow motion,
my favorite,
while I lay on my back and look up,
your favorite.

You can't just stop
worshiping a god,

it don't work that way.

Love t-shirt

At thirteen I fell in love, briefly, with ugly Florian,
the waiter at the Ardéche River Cafe,
eating thickly battered fries and andouille, watching him move like a train
entering its station.
Why couldn't he kiss me? He kept flirting with my sister...

for all of twilight and in the car ride home I thought about burning her hair
up
like a hay-bale,
but that'd be cruel,
so I got drunk under French law, stripped naked, and entertained the family
all night instead.
Sweet revenge,
and yet

Thy Flaming Hearts Brotherhood Customer Support Committee

Sitting there, wilting like a forgotten 7Up in the barn on a hot day.
You're all dirty again, dumb dumb — nobody's fault but your own. Whipped
cream is not for shaving; if anything it's just glue for the kick-back of hay,
huh?
Like a leaf blower to a birthday cake burned by Ina Garten:
aren't you having any fun at all and at the very least
wasn't that funny?
It's a lonely booth in a crowded brothel, to have this body. It's a toilet plate,
flushing condiments — flavor the fish, savor the sushi "That's what my father
always said".

Famished, Arlecchino can find nothing to eat but himself. Starting with
his feet and working up to his knees, thighs, and upper torso, Arlecchino
devours himself.

Late night, the 7UP still there,
rows of horses and their twitching backs,
mostly silent and steaming from the mouth.

While others are speaking, Arlecchino lies on the floor chewing
stones, which seemingly break his teeth and cut his throat.

Speaking with him was like the view from a 50th story Manhattan
apartment, the walls are the television.
Shall I bathe or shall I eat or shall I stare and try to make out shapes?
You're kinda like a TV…

"Why?"
Because you're reflective, fun to watch, and when I put my hand near you it
feels fuzzy."Haha!"

The servant-girl empties a chamber pot out the window. It hits
Pantalone as he serenades Isabella.

Nobody tells jokes anymore:
Have you ever assisted in birthing a cow?
"Haha, no!"

Quick! Bring in the band!
The sound of marching and drums and horns approach in the distance, and
small flashes of colored paper that seems to be spinning and bursting appear,
the smell of matches and lily water intensifying,

Startled, Arlecchino, holding a full glass of wine, executes a com-
plete backward somersault without spilling the wine.

Dancing
is just walking funny and poking ice to the beat with a straw;
these are the agreeable things.
The rotation:
puppy dog eyes, odes to garbage, something actually special, and the squint
of fitting an entire living room inside of your ass, Toe on the ground,
heel lifted,
rotate the ankle,
show the shoe.

"I dare you to drop a house on me", smiling into a cocktail.

Burattino pisses against a rock, from which Zanni appears and embraces Burattino.

I hope I can be one of your best, best buds who you love to have a good time with, that would be so fizzed up.

Thanks, this is good

A monster truck crashes into the bodega's flower display;
the jokes really do write themselves.
He has everything to lose because if the bachelors defeat him they won't just
take his females — they will kill his babies.
Stop smiling like that in the car ride back, stop smiling at all. Haven't you
heard?:
"Chlamydia cousin discovered in deep Arctic Ocean,"
Snow day for all!
Dark rooms, lit by glowing white women drinking and fighting,
this is where we have been hiding.
Not too bad.
A crescendo of quivering strings,
festering between white sofas and beveled edges,
pulsing behind stemless wine glasses and lucite art books;
you couldn't find us if you tried.
"Okay, I'm definitely a Sonja / Bethany hybrid"
"Yeah join the club, bitch"
Licking up the electric green as it splashes out of my
glass.
Thanks, this is good

Sprinkle

At their party
lining a staircase or
wiping the corner of my mouth or
just straight up blown out like birthday candles.
Cold, sweet, smoke,
wrapping around street corners.
Here I am, boys,
ready for my icing and my forks and my car ride home.

An argument

Greasing up the race car — watch it creep
into the shop.

Pulling out his wrench —
watch it click around bolts.

I can smell his sweat through the metal —
he slides out from under the chassis.

Brow rub—
"Um excuse me, do you have anything that's good for sharing?"
"Yeah, I'd recommend the shrimp for two."

Good news it's pre war

The clock on the wall craves transformation.
It craves to be taken down, carried across the kitchen, and tossed in the
washing machine.

That beast of a washing machine
is the thing's whole fantasy.
The door locking shut from the inside,
a hot and heavy cycle,
it's glass wet and fogged,
slicked with detergent,
spinning and hitting the walls of that machine,
that beast of a machine.
It will start slow, and then it will speed up.

Clock jolts out of the daydream,
blushing and fully erect.
It is totally out of it. It has just missed the last five ticks,
and everyone in the world has lost their minds.
The buzzer goes
and the wash cycle comes to a halt.

Village girl hollers from the back:
"Somebody help me! Somebody, please! Help me, please!"
Giant, spider-like man walks into the now-silent kitchen,
he turns his body to fit through the doorway,
a remarkably odd doorway, even for New York.

Waiting on the oven timer now.
Oven is silent.
Butter melts, sprigs of rosemary crisp and shrink,
smells born of heating duck travel through oven door
across the room.

"You sure, cutie?", says countertop,
   he doesn't know it but those were his last words
   to the beautiful things which just moments ago
   were split into pieces on top of him and leaked onto his surface,
   the audibly cold matter which tumbled over him;
   that one cross-eyed onion,
   and those downtown potatoes. It'll be a cold awakening, though a familiar feeling,
   when villain wipes him clean and shuts the lights.
   He'll be there in the dark missing his friends,
   his handsome friends,
   which he is object enough to believe were alive.

   In a past life:
   Some ugly nanny who tortures children
   pours an entire can of coke on the tile floor,
"Clean up this mess you stupid little brat!"
   Lies to the mothers,
   Bedtime at seven
   No to dessert
   Spankings, even,
"We agreed on 200, right?"
   Takes the money,
"Thanks Misses Adler!"
   Later, she will press the elevator button and wait and wait and wait.
   Somewhere,
   there's a spec of dried tomato sauce,
   in it there are traces of once-fresh garlic, oregano, basil, and red chili flakes.
   Where in the world is the tooth, grit or scraper that'll come and chisel it out
   of the grout?

   Where in this life is it?

Fra-go-la

Eff your soup, keep sipping,
it's sweet,

it has some salt and it's
green like the strawberry patch,
it smells like water left sitting in the hose overnight,

you drove it up the driveway and tasted it from a spoon,
you bottled it up and called it
perfume,
when the hose was turned on at 7am,

it pushed out the still water, out came a lizard too,
dead.

As always, he stood there and clapped, big smile guy nodding.
He kissed good though,
so I married his chin, which only a vacuum attachment
could suck on.

Sancerre

Get to work!
Make like a winter apple and crumble,
make like stone fruit in a ramekin and crumble,
make like a cannon and crumble,
make like doggy and beg for treat,
make like me and twirl,
make, like, daddy, like, proud,
make babies!

Five slow ascending xylophone knocks against a pit of Hollywood strings,
everyone deserves dessert.

A ballgame ends, a team swaps states,
and Versailles collapses.
There's juice in you yet

and I'll press it.

Dog Ashes

They spent the long weekend at their aunt's house in Florida eating cold sugar-covered strawberries in the sand, tracing maps of the country with their fingers in sun patches on the carpet. On their last day, groggy, in the late afternoon, their aunt sat them in front of the television and turned on Poltergeist. They cried and screamed. They shivered as the house darkened, they looked at the ground while brushing their teeth.

The following day, the drive home was long and full of crumbs.

Gentle reminder, duck

Remember when we were sitting down and mulling over tassels and mowed-
ways of wearing clips and shirts?

Sitting across from the captain:
New England or Crites,
a clock sat beneath us as a dog shouted from another fairly distant passing
rowboat...

some sky, some olive branch, some thing smoking...

Big

I grew too strong,
and fast,
like a chicken breast shrinks in the oven,
like people die
gloriously
for their little country
that sits on God's beautiful earth.
I saw my reflection and it startled me,
like a fallen leaf
at the nose of a dog.

Concerning the dinner

we don't have Coke,
no Coke or water, just pizza,
that's ok, I'll drink the pizza,
sounds great, I'll be right back!

Epilogue

It was in the reign of George III
that the aforementioned personages lived and quarreled;
good or bad, handsome or ugly, rich or poor
they are all equal now.

(Barry Lyndon, Kubrick, 1975)

Montana James Thomas is a poet based in Manhattan. He is the author of the chapbook, *Pomeranian* (Dirt Children, 2023)

Previously Published:

The Cartoonist, Dirt Child Magazine Volume 4
Beer Battered Slathered in Sauce, Blush Lit Journal
Eloise, Blush Lit Journal (previous version titled *Pretty*)
Dinner Party, Everybody Press Review Issue No. 3
Christian 7th, Everybody Press Review Issue No. 3
Seikilos Epitaph, appeared in chapbook *POMERANIAN* (Dirt Child Press, 2023)
Nothing Left to Watch on TV, appeared in chapbook *POMERANIAN* (Dirt Child Press, 2023)
Thy Flaming Hearts Brotherhood Customer Support Committee, Maudlin House Press
Fra-go-la, Everybody Press Review Issue No. 3
Dog Ashes, appeared in chapbook *POMERANIAN* (Dirt Child Press, 2023)

Artwork:

Jan Weenix. *Still Life with Swan and Game before a Country Estate*, x. 1685, (National Gallery of Art, Washington D.C.)
Grafton, C. B. (1982) *Humorous Victorian Spot Illustrations*. Dover Publications, Inc., pp. 56, 61, 101.

*9 7 9 8 2 1 8 7 4 4 1 3 7 *